P9-DZZ-782

Our Nation's Capital

Activities and Projects for Learning About Washington, D.C.

by Elizabeth F. Russell

FRANKLIN PIERCE
COLLEGE LIBRARY
RINDGE, N.H. 03461

S C H O L A S T I C
PROFESSIONAL BOOKS

New York ✪ Toronto ✪ London ✪ Auckland ✪ Sydney

Dedication
For Stuart, Matthew, and Benjamin—
the lights of my life

Acknowledgments
Thanks to Virginia Dooley for her encouragement,
ideas, patience, and excellent editing;
to Brooke Dojny for her Senate navy bean soup;
and to Paddy Bowman for her help with the Metro.

Teachers may photocopy the designated reproducible pages for classroom use. No other part of this publication may be reproduced in whole or in part, or stored in a retrieval system, or transmitted in any form or by any means electronic, mechanical, photocopying, recording, or otherwise, without written permission of the publisher. For information regarding permission, write to Scholastic Inc., 555 Broadway, New York, NY 10012.

Cover design by Vincent Ceci and Jaime Lucero.

Interior design by Ellen Matlach Hassell
for Boultinghouse & Boultinghouse, Inc.

Interior illustration by Maxie Chambliss,
Ruth Linstromberg, and Manuel Rivera.

Photo research by Cheryl Moch.

Photo Credits
Cover: Steve Vidler/Leo de Wys, Inc.
Interior: p. 53: top, Michael Marsland, Yale University, Office of Public Information; bottom, Mark Antman, The Image Works; p. 54: copyright © MCMXCII Ulrike Welsch/Photo Researchers, Inc.; pp. 1, 4, 11, 12,13, 14, 15, 16, 17, 19, 20, 22, 24, 26, 28, 30, 32, 34, 56: © PhotoDisc, Inc.

ISBN 0-590-59929-1

Copyright © 1996 by Elizabeth F. Russell. All rights reserved.

Printed in the U.S.A.

Contents

Introduction

As a former social studies teacher, I've always loved Washington and have many fond memories of visits to our nation's capital. One visit in particular made me realize how important a "working knowledge" of Washington is to young people's understanding of our government and of our nation's past.

In 1990 my husband and I took our two sons to the capital. On our last afternoon, sixteen-year-old Matt grumbled, "You never took me to the one place I wanted to see." This was the first we knew of his interest in the Vietnam Veterans Memorial. We hopped on the Metro and got off at Arlington. Then it was, "I'm not hiking across that bridge" and "I'm not climbing up those stairs" when I told him there was someone I wanted him to see. We visited Abe Lincoln, yet even that powerful statue didn't move this testy teenager. But then he turned around and looked at the reflecting pool. "Why does this look so familiar?" he asked. When I told him he was standing where Martin Luther King, Jr., had given his "I Have a Dream" speech, Matt's mouth fell open.

After a moment of stunned silence, the questions started to tumble out. Where had I been that August day in 1963? What about Dad? How had the civil rights movement affected us? All that abstract stuff now came alive and connected with his world. More questions followed our walk by the Vietnam Memorial. How many altogether? 58,000. You mean more than everyone in our town? Talk about the teachable moment!

More than ever I realized the importance of connecting the study of American history and government to children's own lives. As a result, the activities in this book evolved into a gentle introduction to the structure and functions of government, connecting the study of Washington's key places, people, and purposes to students' own communities. While the focus of the book is social studies, the activities weave in language arts, math, science, art, and music. The wide variety of activities accommodates different ability levels and learning styles. The book has a flexible structure. You can pick and choose those places and people you want to explore with your students.

I hope *Our Nation's Capital* opens up many teachable moments for you and your students. Above all, have fun with it!

Elizabeth F. Russell

Washington in the Beginning

Background Information

The Land Itself

Long before it became the nation's capital, the area around Washington, D.C., was a natural meeting place. Here two rivers meet—the Potomac and the Anacostia. Here, too, the harder rocks of the Piedmont meet the softer rocks of the Atlantic coastal plain. And perhaps foreshadowing a future compromise, trees of the northern woodlands, such as elms, oaks, chestnuts, and beeches, meet southern pines, walnuts, and poplars.

Before it was developed into a city, this area was mostly low-lying and wet. Its waters teemed with fish, and marshes of wild rice covered the estuary of the Anacostia River. The riverbanks were home to Canadian geese, canvasback ducks, blue herons, beavers, otters, frogs, toads, and box tortoises. In the woods lived animals large and small—bears, deer, elks, cougars, wildcats, wolves, wild turkeys, golden eagles, red and gray foxes, raccoons, opossums, minks, skunks, weasels, muskrats, flying squirrels, chipmunks, and woodchucks. Growing wild were blueberries, huckleberries, wild celery, and sassafras.

The First Inhabitants

The Piscataway were the first people to live here. They came from the Nanticoke people on the eastern shore of Maryland and were members of the Algonquian family of tribes, northern relations of the Powhatan, the tribe of Pocahontas. The Piscataway lived near the rivers in villages, fishing, hunting, and also farming their food. From the riverbanks they got clay for pots and reeds for baskets. They quarried rock and made stone implements. According to tradition, they used the river in the valley at the foot of what is now Capitol Hill for fishing grounds and held their council gatherings at Greenleaf Point not far away.

Captain John Smith, of Jamestown fame, explored this region in 1608 and wrote the following descriptions of Native American life.

Their buildings are for the most part by the river or not far distant from some fresh spring of water. Their houses are built like our arbors, of small young branches, bowed and tied, and so closely covered with mats or the bark of trees, that both in wind and rain they are warm as stoves, but very smoky. Yet at the top of the house there is a hole made for the smoke.

Their houses are in the midst of their fields, which are of 20, 40, 100, and 200 acres. Sometimes from 2 to 100 of these houses are together.

The women make mats, baskets, pots, mortars, pound their corn, make their bread, prepare their food, plant their corn, gather their corn, bear all kinds of burdens, and such like.

The greatest labor they take is in planting their corn, for the country naturally is overgrown with wood. To prepare the ground they bruise the bark of the trees near the root. Then they do scorch the roots with fire so they grow no more.

In March and April they live much upon their fishing and feed on fish, turkeys, and squirrels. In May and June they plant their fields and live mostly on acorns, walnuts, and fish.

Their fishing is much in boats. These they make of one tree by burning.

From Wilderness to Washington

By 1675, the Piscataway had left this area and moved up the Potomac River to escape the Europeans who were taking over the land. English settlers had begun arriving in the Potomac area in 1634, and by the 1700s the area was divided into large estates and farms.

After the American Revolution, Northern and Southern states argued bitterly over where to locate the new nation's capital. Finally, Thomas Jefferson and Alexander Hamilton struck a deal—the Northern states agreed to a site on the Potomac River, and the Southern states agreed to have the federal government pay states' war debts. In 1790 Congress approved a ten-mile square carved out of Maryland and Virginia to be called the District of Columbia, in honor of Christopher Columbus. Within this square, George Washington knew just the location he wanted for the city, for he had camped there overnight as a young surveyor. Wasting no time, he hired an enthusiastic young Frenchman, Pierre-Charles L'Enfant, to draw up plans for the capital. The national government was to take up residence there in 1800.

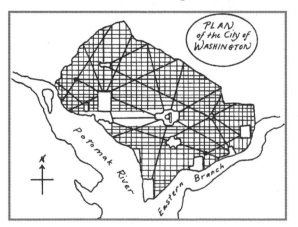

L'Enfant envisioned an elegant city. On Jenkin's Hill he planned the Capitol building itself, and northwest of it in an orchard he placed the President's House, as he called it. Connecting the two buildings would be a broad boulevard, one of many he had planned. But L'Enfant's dreams outstripped the pocketbook of the young nation and overstepped the democratic vision of its leaders. When he refused to make any changes to his design, he was fired and took his plans with him. Fortunately his surveyor, an African American mathematician named Benjamin Banneker, was able to draw the map from memory.

Work on the nation's capital moved ahead slowly. On Columbus Day in 1792, the cornerstone of the President's House was laid, and eleven months later Washington himself laid the cornerstone of the north wing of the Capitol. By 1800, neither building was completed. Nor was the Treasury building or the War Office, but the federal government moved from Philadelphia to Washington anyway. The new nation and its new capital city were both beginning to take shape.

Activities

Setting the Stage

Display a map of the United States and ask students to name and locate our nation's capital. Discuss why Washington is important: It's the home of our national government and site of many places honoring important people and events in our nation's history. Ask students what they already know about Washington, D.C., and write their responses on chart paper under the heading *What We Know.*

What We Know	What We Want to Find Out	What We Learned

Next, have students brainstorm all the things they would like to know about Washington. List these under *What We Want to Find Out.* Encourage each student to contribute a question. If students have difficulty, suggest a few to loosen them up. For example, How many children have lived in the White House? How tall is the Washington Monument? How much money is printed every day?

As students work through the activities in this unit, have them record what they find out on a separate sheet labeled *What We Learned.* (Students might like to decorate it in red, white, and blue.)

Living on the Land

Ask students to imagine themselves in a new land with absolutely none of their modern conveniences. Discuss the kinds of things they'd need to survive—food, clothing, shelter—and how they could go about getting them. Now distribute copies of page 9 and tell students that the land on which Washington is built looked something like this when Native Americans lived there. Ask them to predict everything that could be used for food with an F, for clothing with a C, and for shelter with an S.

Have students compare their predictions. Then read aloud to students John Smith's description of how Native Americans lived on the land (page 5) and have them see how close their predictions came.

 Writing Connection Ask students to use what they've seen and heard to write directions for building a shelter or preparing a meal.

 Science Connection Ask students what kind of habitat is shown on the reproducible. Suggest that they draw a picture of the food chain in this environment, then explain how the different elements are dependent on one another.

 Hometown Connection What did your area look like 400 years ago? Did Native Americans live there? If so, how did they meet their basic needs? If no one lived there, why not? How could you find answers to these questions? Students can visit the local library or museum or write to your state historical society for information. How did life in your area compare to life in the Washington area?

Washington Walk-About

Unlike most cities in the world, Washington, D.C., was planned before it was built. The map on page 10 shows the heart of the city designed by Pierre-Charles L'Enfant. Photocopy page 10 and distribute it to students. Have students use the compass rose and scale to answer the questions and find their way around Washington. When everyone's done, compare answers. Encourage students to make up their own walk-about questions for their friends. For example: Start at the Lincoln Memorial and walk one mile east. Then turn south and go one-half mile. Go east again for another half mile. Where are you?

Answers to Student Worksheet: (1) Washington Monument (2) Capitol (3) northwest (4) Lincoln Memorial; about 1½ miles (5) southeast; 1 mile; There's water (Tidal Basin) in the way.

 Math Connection Choose a big space, the school gym if possible, where students can enlarge this map. Then have students measure the length and width of the area and calculate the scale they would need to use to draw the map. (Hint: It's about 2.5 miles from the Lincoln Memorial to the Capitol, or 13,200 feet.) Students should draw the main features of the map to scale, using markers on kraft paper, tape on the floor, or colored chalk on the playground. Interested students might get a complete map of Washington and add streets to the scale drawing.

 Hometown Connection Ask students to draw a map of their neighborhood or town, to scale if possible. They should show their home, their school, and other important buildings. Suggest that they find out why your community is located where it is, when it was founded, why it was founded, and by whom.

BOOK LINKS

- *City! Washington, D.C.* by Shirley Climo (Macmillan, 1991). Informative text and full-color photos detail the rich and distinctive history and attractions in our capital.

- *Encyclopedia of Native American Tribes* by Carl Waldman (Facts on File, 1988). Although titled an encyclopedia, this book is extremely readable. Topics covered under "Algonquian" include social structure, food, houses, transportation, clothing, other arts and crafts, and religion.

INTERNET SITE

- Get a full-color interactive map of Washington, D.C. Important sites are hot-linked to pages of information.

     http://sc94.ameslab.gov:80/TOUR/tour.html

Name _____

Living on the Land

The Native Americans who lived in the Washington, D.C., area were called the Piscataway. They were part of the Algonquian family of nations and used the resources of the land to live. This picture shows many of those resources.

Look carefully at the picture, then write F on each thing you think they used for food, C on each thing they used for clothing, and S on each thing they used for shelter. (Some things could have more than one use.)

Washington Walk-About

Here is the heart of the capital city planned by Pierre-Charles L'Enfant. You can see the wide avenues he designed and the Mall where he intended to place statues honoring American heroes. How many famous buildings can you locate on this map? Use the compass rose and the scale to answer the questions.

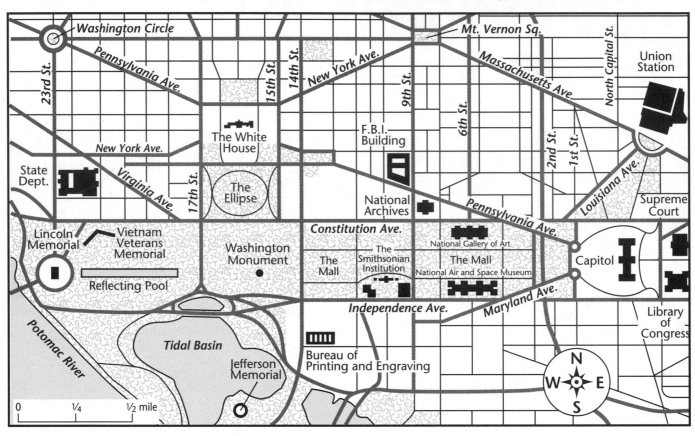

1. Walk due south from the White House. Which famous monument do you find? _____

   _____

2. Now walk east for about a mile and half. Where are you? _____

3. From there walk over to the Federal Bureau of Investigation. In which direction did you

   walk? _____

4. Now walk south to the Mall and turn west. Walk to the building at the west end of the

   Mall. What is it? _____ About how far did you walk? _____

5. If you could walk *directly* from this building to the Jefferson Memorial, in which direction

   would you go? How long a walk would it be? Why can't you walk that way? _____

   _____

Some of Washington's Important Places

Background Information

Washington, D.C., has been called "America's hometown" because it belongs to all of us. The activities and reproducibles in this section of the book help students get to know some of the most important places in our nation's capital—their stories, what they look like, and what purpose they serve. As they learn about these places, students will get a feel for some of the governmental and cultural activities of the city.

From there it's an easy step to look at the workings of government and the use of public space in your own community. The following activities contain suggestions not only for learning more about Washington and the federal government but also for linking that knowledge to students' immediate world. Students will see that government at any level provides for public safety and public services. Through their inquiries, students will also come to see that different levels of government handle different types of issues.

In this section there are suggested activities, cross-curricular connections, and book and Internet links for ten of Washington's important places. The reproducibles on pages 20–35 provide students with background information and models of eight of these places. All of the models are easy to make: students color, cut out, and attach the buildings to folded cardboard or empty juice or milk cartons using paste or tape. Encourage students to do the Try This activities on the student background information page.

Activities

Model City

You might want to have students work in cooperative groups as they make their models. Each group can set up its own mini-Washington, using the map from "Washington Walk-About" (page 10) as a guide for placement of buildings. Or if the class drew a map to scale in that activity, have students arrange their buildings on it.

This is a good time to discuss why these important places are all grouped together instead of spread out all over Washington, D.C. Ask students what

makes a place special. Why do we want to make the center of our government a special place? Where are the government buildings in your community? Why are they there? What feelings does this public space create?

Host a "D.C. Day"

After students have made their models, hold a "D.C. Day" where they can display their models and tell about the buildings. Serve refreshments using the recipes on pages 20 and 22 to make it really special.

White House

After students have read the background information on page 20, suggest that they write a letter to the President telling him one important thing they'd like him to do. They'll even get an answer! The President's address is:

> The White House
> 1600 Pennsylvania Avenue
> Washington, D.C. 20500

 Writing Connection Have students find out what the president does. Students can follow the news for a week and come up with a list of the president's responsibilities. Ask students to write a want ad for president, including the qualifications they think are needed for the job. They might also enjoy writing about what they would do if they were president of the United States.

 Hometown Connection Remind students that the president must see that the laws of the nation are carried out. Who has this executive job in your local government? How did this person get the job? How is it like the president's job? How is it different? Students can visit your mayor or city manager to learn about his or her responsibilities.

BOOK LINKS

✪ *Dear Chelsea* edited by Judy Goldberg (Scholastic, 1994). Children's letters to Chelsea Clinton, with lots of interesting facts about life in the White House.

✪ *Growing Up in the White House* by Seymour Reit (Macmillan, 1968). Anecdotes of all of the children who've lived in the White House, from the Adams grandchildren to the Johnson girls. Also good general information on the presidents.

✪ *The Last Cow on the White House Lawn & Other Little-Known Facts About the Presidency* by Barbara Seuling (Doubleday, 1978). Fascinating presidential trivia.

✪ *The White House* by Leonard Everett Fisher (Holiday House, 1989). Illustrated description of historical development of the White House and of its occupants.

INTERNET SITE

✪ <u>Welcome to the White House</u> Hyperlinked information on the president and vice president; Interactive Citizens' Handbook; White House history and tours; a virtual library of documents, speeches, and photos; the Briefing Room on current topics; a White House Help Desk; and The White House for Kids, which has a section on Historic Moments of the Presidency and a magazine called *Inside the White House* with explanations of current issues facing the federal government written in kid-friendly language.

   http://www2.whitehouse.gov/WH/Welcome-nt.html

Capitol

Encourage students to find out how many representatives their state sends to work in the Capitol and to find out which one represents the district they live in. Who are their senators? Ask them to create a chart that shows who their representatives and senators are and when they will be up for reelection.

 Civics Connection To simulate the workings of Congress, have students discuss what kind of law they would like to have. Choose one of the students' suggestions, making sure it's a general idea. Divide the class into the Senate and the House of Representatives and ask each group to discuss the idea and agree on a specific way to make it a law. (Each group should have a discussion leader and one person to write the final "bill.") Next have groups compare their bills and work out any differences, then vote. From there the bill would go on to the president to be signed into law or vetoed.

 Hometown Connection Ask students to find out who makes the laws for your community. How do these people get the job? What kinds of laws do they pass? How are they different from the laws that Congress passes? If possible, have a member of the City Council come and speak to the class.

INTERNET SITES

✪ <u>The Capitol Building</u> http://www.dcpages.com/Hwdc/capitol.html

✪ <u>Electronic Activist</u> E-mail address directory of congresspeople, state governments, and media entities.

   http://berkshire.net/~ifas/activist

✪ <u>How to Contact Members of Congress</u>

   http://www.we.com/lgc/howmail.html

✪ <u>A Layperson's Guide to Congress</u> Describes briefly how Congress works.

   http://www.we.com/lgc/

Supreme Court

Invite students to find out who our current Supreme Court Justices are and when they were appointed. Tell them that on the east side of the Supreme Court building are the words "Justice the Guardian of Liberty" and statues of Moses, Confucius, and Solon. Ask students to work in three groups to find out who these three men were and what they have to do with justice. Have the groups share their findings with the class.

 Science Connection Tell students that one of the statues at the Supreme Court is blindfolded and holds a balance scale. Have students research how a balance scale works. What does it have to do with justice? And why is the figure blindfolded?

 Hometown Connection Have students locate the courthouse in your community. Who is the judge? What goes on at a trial? Invite a judge to talk with your class and, if possible, go to visit his or her courtroom.

BOOK LINKS

✪ *Sandra Day O'Connor: First Woman on the Supreme Court* by Carol Greene (Children's Press, 1982). Biography.

✪ *The Supreme Court* by Carol Greene (Children's Press, 1985). Describes the function and structure of the Supreme Court, together with a brief overview of some important cases and well-known justices. For younger readers.

✪ *The Supreme Court* by Ann E. Weiss (Enslow, 1987). A history of the Supreme Court presented through selected cases. For older readers.

INTERNET SITE

✪ Justices of the Supreme Court Photo of all justices, links to individual photos and biographies.

    http://www.law.cornell.edu/supct/justices/fullcourt.html

Smithsonian Institution

On August 10, 1846, Congress completed the Act of Establishment which founded the Smithsonian Institution. What started more than 150 years ago as a natural history museum has grown into the world's largest museum and research complex. Today the institution encompasses research facilities, observatories, libraries, and 16 museums. It even has traveling exhibitions that visit cities throughout the U.S. Explain to students that their model shows the part of the Smithsonian called "the castle."

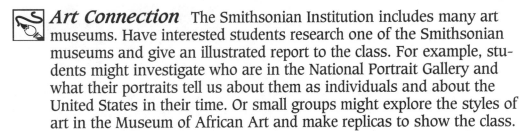

Art Connection The Smithsonian Institution includes many art museums. Have interested students research one of the Smithsonian museums and give an illustrated report to the class. For example, students might investigate who are in the National Portrait Gallery and what their portraits tell us about them as individuals and about the United States in their time. Or small groups might explore the styles of art in the Museum of African Art and make replicas to show the class.

Music Connection The Smithsonian Institution's Office of Folklife Programs administers Folkways Recordings, music and spoken words from around the world. Among its vast collection are historical and political songs of the United States. You can enliven your study of Washington, D.C., with old election songs or songs of the American Revolution or the War of 1812, when the British burned Washington. There's even a recording of American history told through its folk songs. Many Folkways Recordings are available in public libraries. For a catalog, write to Smithsonian/Folkways Recordings, Office of Folklife Programs, 955 L'Enfant Plaza, Washington, D.C. 20560.

Hometown Connection How do we know about the past? What artifacts give us the best information about how people lived long ago? Students can practice the crafts of the historian and the curator by researching the history of your school and preparing a display for the school library. When was the school built? How did it get its name? What did the first students wear? What kinds of games did they play? Did they study the same things as students today? Did any famous people attend this school? Have students look for old photos, old school newspapers and clippings from the local newspaper, and interviews with teachers and former students.

BOOK LINK

✪ *The Story of the Smithsonian Institution* by R. Conrad Stein (Children's Press, 1974). How a British scientist endowed one of America's greatest cultural treasures.

INTERNET SITES

✪ National Museum of Natural History Take a tour of the museum, illustrated with lots of photographs.

> http://si.edu/organiza/museums/nmnh/start.html

✪ National Air and Space Museum Floor plan of each floor of the museum. Click on a gallery to view its contents. Unbelievably cool!

> http://www.nasm.edu/NASMAP.html

Memorials: Jefferson, Lincoln, Vietnam Veterans, and Washington Monument

After students have read the background information on the Jefferson, Lincoln, Vietnam Veterans memorials, and the Washington Monument, have them make a giant time line to show important events in American history. Use adding-machine tape and let one inch stand for one year. Decide how many years back in time you want your time line to go, then measure out enough paper. Below are some dates to get students started. Have them add more dates as they learn about Washington, D.C. Be sure they include when they were born.

1776	1861	1920	1963
Declaration of Independence	Civil War starts	Women get the right to vote	Dr. King's "I Have a Dream" speech

1750   1800   1850   1900   1950   2000

 Hometown Connection Ask students who is honored by a statue, a monument, or a building in your community. Why is this person important to remember?

BOOK LINKS

✪ *Meet Thomas Jefferson* by Marvin Barrett (Random House, 1967). An introduction to the third President for younger readers.

✪ *A Picture Book of Thomas Jefferson* by David A. Adler (Holiday House, 1990). Describes Jefferson's life and achievements.

✪ *Thomas Jefferson: A Picture Book Biography* by James Giblin (Scholastic, 1994). Excellent text accompanies pictures.

✪ *A Memorial for Mr. Lincoln* by Brent Ashabranner (Putnam, 1992). Describes Lincoln's role in American history and the planning and building of the Lincoln Memorial.

✪ *George Washington: A Picture Book* by James Giblin (Scholastic, 1992). Examines Washington's family life, careers, and myths and legends about him. Also describes monuments to Washington and Mount Vernon.

✪ *A Picture Book of George Washington* by David A. Adler (Holiday House, 1989). Important events in Washington's life, told for younger readers.

✪ *A Wall of Names: The Story of the Vietnam Veterans Memorial* by Judy Donnelly (Random House, 1991). Surveys the history of the Vietnam War, chronicles the construction of the Vietnam Veterans Memorial, and discusses what the memorial means to many Americans.

INTERNET SITES

✪ Lincoln Memorial Color photo, hot links to information on Abraham Lincoln, the Gettysburg Address, and Lincoln's assassination.

> http://sc94.ameslab.gov/TOUR/linmem.html

✪ Washington Monument Color photo, history of the building, link to a portrait and biography of George Washington.

> http://sc94.ameslab.gov/TOUR/washmon.html

✪ Personal Legacy An exhibit of things left at the wall.

> http://photo2si.edu/legacy/legacylinks.html

Bureau of Engraving and Printing/Treasury Department

At the Bureau of Engraving and Printing, our paper money is printed—about $22.5 million every day! The Bureau also prints postage stamps, passports, and other government certificates, but most visitors are interested in the money.

You can watch money being printed. The special paper is made from cloth, 75% cotton and 25% linen, and has red and blue fibers running through it to show that the money is genuine, not counterfeit. It takes from one to three days to print a $1 bill. The average dollar stays in circulation for about 18 months.

Our paper money has both pictures and symbols honoring our government and past leaders. Have students find out who appears on the front of the $5 bill, the $10 bill, $20 bill, and $50 bill. Then have them find out what buildings are on the backs of these bills. ($5—Abraham Lincoln/Lincoln Memorial; $10—Alexander Hamilton/U.S. Treasury; $20—Andrew Jackson/the White House; $50—Ulysses S. Grant/the U.S. Capitol)

It is unconstitutional for states or communities to create their own money. But just for the fun of it, invite students to design their own paper money. What pictures and symbols should they use?

 Civics Connection Have students find out why only the federal government can print and mint currency. What do they think would happen if every state had its own money?

 Hometown Connection Take a class trip to your local bank and learn what the bank does with money people deposit.

BOOK LINK

✪ *Money, Money, Money* by Nancy Winslow Parker (Harper, 1995). The meaning of the art and symbols on U.S. paper currency. Fascinating!

INTERNET SITES

✪ Printing Money How the Bureau of Engraving and Printing produces dollar bills (Newton's Apple Show #1212).

> http://ericir.syr.edu/Newton/Lessons/money.html

✪ United States Treasury Bureau of Engraving and Printing From this home page, you can access a 30-second video, "Money Hot Off the Press," of how currency is printed, and a 39-second video with sound, "The Making of Money."

> http://www.ustreas.gov/treasury/bureaus/bep/bep.html

National Archives

The National Archives is an enormous building in which all the nation's important documents—treaties, photographs, movies, and more—are stored. There are documents dating as far back as 1775! The old documents need to be protected. The original Declaration of Independence, Constitution, and the Bill of Rights, for example, are stored in glass cases filled with helium. The public can view them during the day. At night the documents are lowered into underground chambers.

One of the most interesting things to do at the National Archives is to trace a family's history. Using census records, immigration information, and other documents, you can follow a family back in time and learn where its ancestors came from. Invite students to create a family tree for their own family using the form on page 36. (You may want to skip this activity if you think it will upset any students in your class.)

 Hometown Connection The National Archives has a wealth of information, from census records to lists of ships' passengers, military records, tax rolls, naturalization records—everything you can think of and a lot more. Many communities have genealogical societies. Invite a genealogist to visit your class and explain how students can use local archives to find out about an ancestor.

 Writing Connection Have students discover all they can about an ancestor and write a short biography. If you live near one of the eleven field branches of the National Archives, students can investigate their holdings. Local libraries might provide other important resources, such as census records on microfilm and local family histories.

INTERNET SITE

✪ National Archives Online Exhibit Hall Illustrated and annotated exhibits: Tokens and Treasures (gifts to 12 presidents), American Originals (primary sources), Charters of Freedom (Big 3: Declaration of Independence, Constitution, Bill of Rights), Powers of Persuasion (World War II poster art), District of Columbia Emancipation Act, A Day in the Life of the President. Extraordinary.

http://www.nara.gov/edxhall/exhibits.html

The White House

"I never forget that the house I live in belongs to all the people," said President Franklin D. Roosevelt. The White House has been home to all of the presidents and their families since 1800. It's also where the president has his office and entertains important leaders from around the world.

The first First Family to live there was John and Abigail Adams, but the President's House wasn't finished when they moved in. "We have not the least fence, yard or other convenience," wrote Mrs. Adams. She even had to use the East Room to dry the laundry! The next President, Thomas Jefferson, completed the building and also introduced many new things to his guests, including macaroni, waffles, and ice cream.

It wasn't always called the White House. During the War of 1812, the British burned down the President's House. When it was rebuilt, workers covered the scorch marks with many coats of white paint. From then on, it was known informally as the White House

until President Teddy Roosevelt made the name official in 1901.

If you lived in the White House, you'd expect to be on your best behavior all the time. But presidential children have found ways to have fun there too. Once (and only once!) President Garfield's son Irwin rode his bicycle down the marble staircase and round and round the East Room. When Archie Roosevelt had the measles, Teddy Roosevelt's other children smuggled their pony into the White House to cheer him up. President Taft's children loved "tray-sliding" down the marble staircase and looking for the ghosts of Abraham Lincoln and Abigail Adams.

More than a million people visit the White House each year, for it is a treasure-house of American history.

Try This

Make a tasty version of the dessert Thomas Jefferson introduced at the White House, chocolate ice cream.

Chocolate Ice Cream

1 can (14 ounces) sweetened condensed milk
2/3 cup chocolate syrup
1 pint (2 cups) heavy cream

2 mixing bowls
eggbeater (or electric mixer, with adult only)
spoon
9" × 5" loaf pan, lined with aluminum foil

Mix together the sweetened condensed milk and chocolate syrup in a mixing bowl. In another bowl, whip the cream until it is stiff. Then fold the whipped cream into the chocolate mixture and pour it into the loaf pan. Cover the top with foil and put it in the freezer. When it is firm, peel off the foil and enjoy. Makes about 1½ quarts of ice cream.

White House

Color and cut out the White House. Prop it up with cardboard or a juice box. Then "landscape" the grounds around it. Add this to a model of our nation's capital.

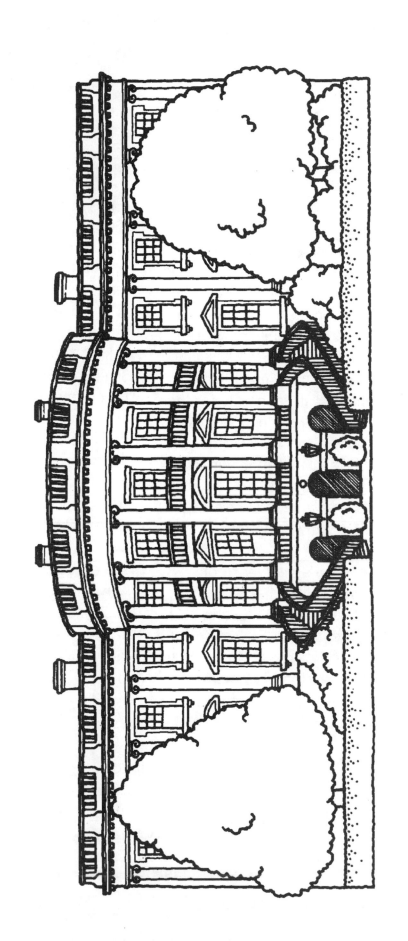

The Capitol

The Capitol is the second oldest building in the capital. What's the difference between the capital and the Capitol? The city of Washington is our nation's capital, the center of our federal government. The Capitol is the building where Congress meets. Look at the Capitol's huge round dome. The round dome will remind you to spell the building, not the city, with an o.

George Washington and Pierre-Charles L'Enfant chose Jenkin's Hill as the site for the Capitol in 1791. They wanted people to see the "Congress House" from all over the city. L'Enfant placed this building at the very center of his design, with avenues spreading out from it like spokes on a wheel. To this day, going to "the Hill" means going to Congress.

What is Congress? It's the branch of our federal government that makes laws. Congress has two parts, the Senate and the House of Representatives. Each state sends two senators to Congress. The House of Representatives has 435 members. The number of representatives each state sends to the House depends on the size of its population. Do you know how many representatives your state has?

More than 10 million people visit the Capitol every year to see democracy in action. You can watch a session of the Senate or House with a pass from your senator or representative. As the showplace of our nation's government, the Capitol has lots of interesting things to see—huge bronze doors showing scenes in the life of Christopher Columbus, murals of American history, statues of famous people, and even columns carved with tobacco leaves and ears of corn.

Try This

It's an old tradition in both the Senate and House restaurants to have bean soup on the menu every day. In fact, it's even an order of Congress! Here's an easy version to make and enjoy when it's chilly outside.

Senate Navy Bean Soup

8 cups water
6 cups canned navy (or other white) beans
2 cups chopped onions
1 medium potato, peeled and chopped
2 carrots, chopped
2 stalks celery, chopped
2 cloves garlic, chopped
1 bay leaf
1 cup tomato sauce
1 teaspoon salt
$\frac{1}{4}$ teaspoon black pepper

large pot
mixing spoon
eggbeater
mixing bowl

Place water, beans, vegetables, and bay leaf in pot. Simmer uncovered for 30–40 minutes. When vegetables are very tender, add tomato sauce, salt, and pepper. Discard bay leaf. Put half the soup in bowl. Beat until smooth. Return it to pot to thicken the soup. Taste it and adjust seasonings. Good stuff!

The Capitol

Color and cut out the Capitol.
Prop it up with cardboard or a juice box and
add it to your model of our nation's capital.

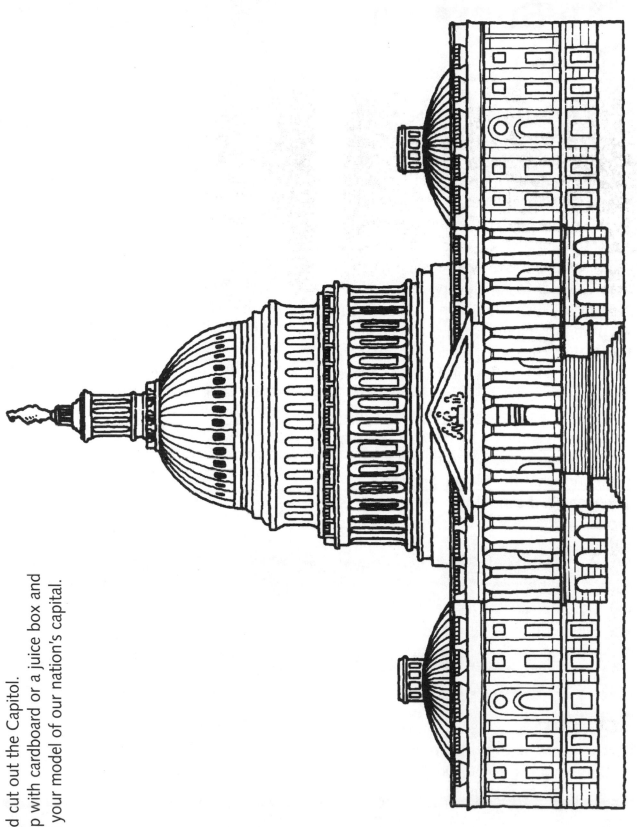

The Supreme Court

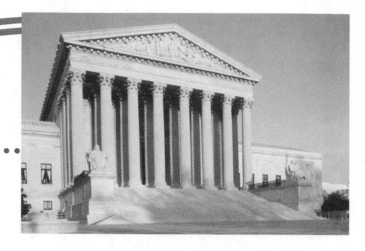

"Equal Justice Under Law." These words appear over the big bronze front doors of the Supreme Court. The job of the Court is to see that the laws of our country provide fair protection to everyone.

The Supreme Court is the highest court in our country. It has nine judges, called justices, and one is the Chief Justice. They meet from October to April every year to hear legal cases. Even though thousands of cases are brought to them, the justices choose only about 150. They must decide whether state laws, acts of Congress, and actions of the President are constitutional.

What does *constitutional* mean? The Constitution is the highest law of the land. It tells how the federal government is organized and what the federal and state governments can and cannot do, and it protects people's rights.

One of the most important Supreme Court decisions was *Brown v. Board of Education* in 1954. The Court ruled that having separate schools for black and white children was unconstitutional. In its decision, the Court said that education "is a right which must be made available to all on equal terms." Therefore, separating children by race deprives African American children of equal protection of the laws guaranteed by the Constitution.

The style of the Supreme Court building comes from ancient Greece and Rome. The United States gets some its ideas of democracy from the Greeks and of law from the Romans.

Try This

❂ The Supreme Court hears many cases throughout the year. Do you have a case you'd like to present? Is there something at your school you feel is unfair? Should recess be longer? Should the cafeteria serve different food? Prepare a case to present to your class. Be sure to give specific reasons why you think a change should be made.

❂ The lawyer who won *Brown v. Board of Education* was Thurgood Marshall. Later he became the first African American Supreme Court justice. Find out more about him and make a poster that tells about his life.

The Supreme Court

Color, cut out, and prop up the Supreme Court. Add it to your scale model of Washington. Where does it stand in relation to the Capitol?

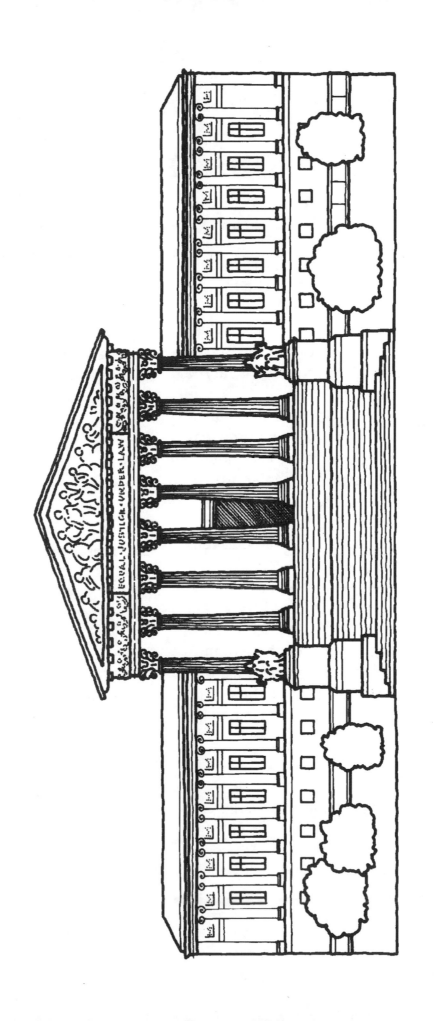

EQUAL · JUSTICE · UNDER · LAW

The Smithsonian Institution

What would you do if someone left you $550,000 in his will and said you had to use it for "an establishment for the increase and diffusion [spreading] of knowledge"? What kind of knowledge—science? history? sports? And how to spread it—a school? a library? a laboratory? a museum?

That's the dilemma Congress faced after James Smithson died in 1829. Smithson was a British scientist who wanted to promote learning. But he'd never even visited the United States! Finally, after much debate, Congress decided in 1846 to use the money to set up the Smithsonian Institution to carry out scientific research.

Since then, the Smithsonian has expanded from a single laboratory to include more than a dozen organizations that do research and educate the public about everything from dinosaur bones to fine arts to space flight.

In the National Museum of Natural History, you can see the largest diamond in the world and the skull of a fish 350 million years old that was as big as a horse. Next door is "America's attic"—the National Museum of American History. There you can find treasures like George Washington's army uniform, the original star-spangled banner, and the inaugural gowns of many first ladies. The National Gallery of Art holds master-pieces from around the world. By far the most popular part of the Smithsonian is the National Air and Space Museum. In it you'll see everything related to flight from the Wright brothers' first airplane to a duplicate of the *Apollo* moon landing module. It even has a moon rock you can touch!

Your model is of the Smithsonian's first home on the Mall in Washington. Today this building is the headquarters for all parts of the Smithsonian Institution.

Try This

- How did people learn to make flying machines? Research this subject in your school or public library. Then with your classmates create a mural showing the history of flight.

- Lots of Smithsonian exhibits show us how people lived at different times and in different places. Did you ever think about how people of the future will know us? Make a time capsule showing life today, then bury it for future generations to discover. What do you think should be the most important things to show?

The Smithsonian Institution

Color and cut out the Smithsonian "Castle." Prop it up with cardboard or a juice box and add it to your model of our nation's capital.

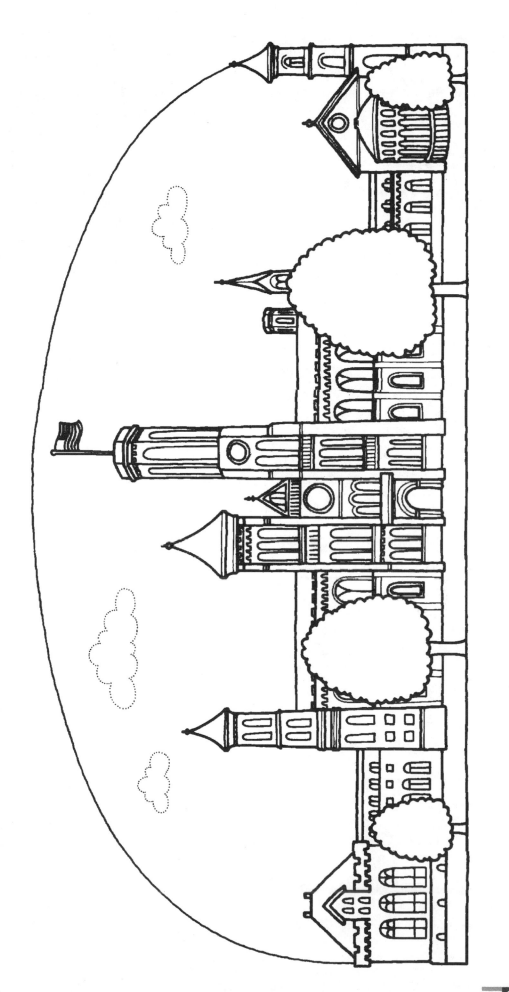

Lincoln Memorial

Four score and seven years ago our fathers brought forth on this continent, a new nation, conceived in Liberty, and dedicated to the proposition that all men are created equal. . . .

On a sunny day in November 1863, President Abraham Lincoln began to speak. Lincoln had traveled from Washington to Gettysburg, Pennsylvania, to dedicate a cemetery for soldiers. In his speech he paid tribute to the soldiers who had died to uphold America's ideals of freedom and equality.

At that time the United States was fighting the terrible Civil War. The Northern states of the Union battled to keep the Southern states from splitting apart and forming a separate country. As President, Lincoln kept the Union together. During the war he also freed the slaves.

For these two great accomplishments—preserving the Union and ending slavery—the Lincoln Memorial honors our sixteenth President. The building looks like a temple in ancient Greece, where democracy began. Around the outside are 36 columns, one for each state when Lincoln was President. Broad stone steps lead up to a 19-foot-tall statue of the Great Emancipator, as Lincoln was called. You can read the words of the Gettysburg Address on one wall.

One hundred years after Lincoln freed the slaves, another great leader came to Washington to speak to a large crowd. Standing on the steps of the Lincoln Memorial, Dr. Martin Luther King, Jr., called on all Americans to turn our nation's ideals into reality for everyone:

I have a dream my four little children will one day live in a nation where they will not be judged by the color of their skin but by the content of their character.

Try This

✪ Read more about Abraham Lincoln and Martin Luther King, Jr. Then imagine that they could talk with each other. What do you think they'd say? With a friend, act out this conversation.

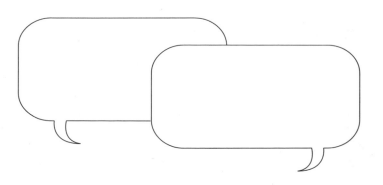

Lincoln Memorial

Color and cut out the Lincoln Memorial. Prop it up with cardboard or a juice box and add it to your model of our nation's capital.

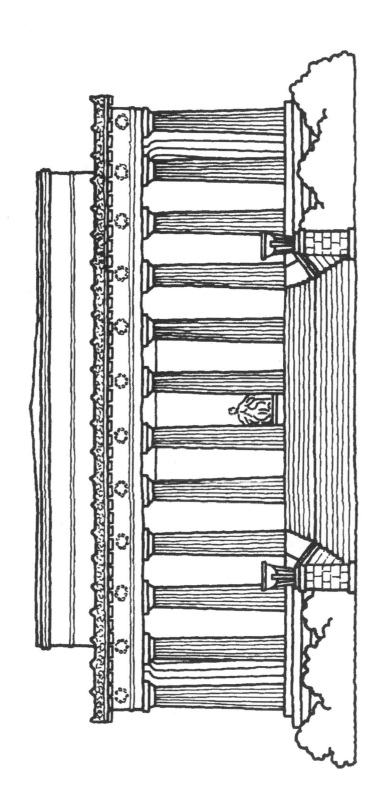

Jefferson Memorial

We hold these truths to be self-evident, that all men are created equal, that they are endowed by their Creator with certain inalienable Rights, that among these are Life, Liberty and the pursuit of Happiness.

These words from the Declaration of Independence state the most important ideas on which our government is based. In 1776 Thomas Jefferson wrote the Declaration to tell King George III and the world why the American colonies were breaking away from Great Britain. His words remain the cornerstone of American democracy today.

The Jefferson Memorial honors Thomas Jefferson not only for writing the Declaration of Independence but also for his life of public service. He was minister to France, secretary of state for George Washington, and third President of the United States. As President, he doubled the size of the new nation by adding millions of acres from the Mississippi River to the Rocky Mountains.

The original Constitution provided that every four years five men could run for president. Whoever received the most electoral votes would become president, and the person with the next most votes would be vice president. (This wasn't a very good idea. These two people might be enemies.) In the election of 1800, Jefferson and Aaron Burr received the same number of votes! The decision was left to the House of Representatives, who voted to make Jefferson President and Burr Vice President.

More than a statesman, Jefferson was also the leading architect of his time, a scientific farmer, a musician, and an inventor. Did you know that he invented the swivel chair?

Try This

- ✪ What do you think is really unfair? What do you want to be free from? Write your own declaration of independence. Be sure to give solid reasons to support your position.

- ✪ Jefferson invented many things—everything from revolving clothes racks in his closet to our coinage system of dollars and cents. What problem could you solve with an invention? Go ahead and make it! Have a class inventions day to honor Thomas Jefferson, perhaps on April 13, his birthday.

Jefferson Memorial

Color and cut out the Jefferson Memorial. Prop it up with cardboard or a juice box and add it to your model of our nation's capital.

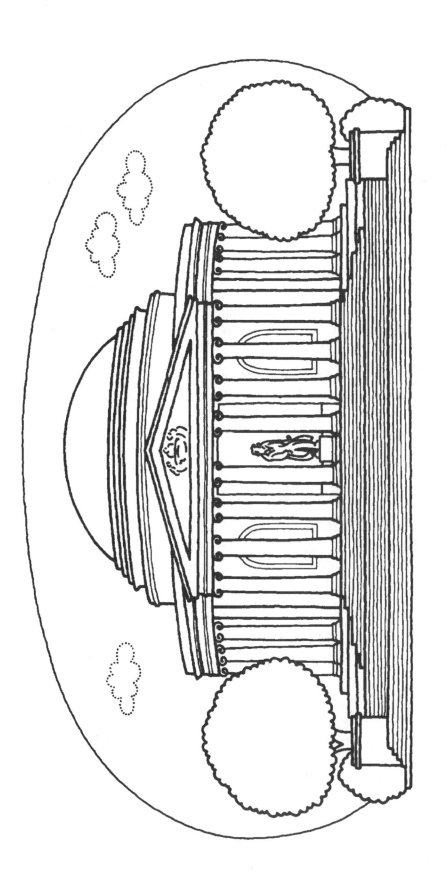

Vietnam Veterans Memorial

"It just overwhelms you," said a former Marine sergeant when he first saw the Vietnam Veterans Memorial in Washington. Dedicated in 1982, it is one of the newest and most moving monuments in America. Two black granite walls form a V that slopes down into the Mall. On these walls are inscribed the names of the more than 58,000 Americans who died (or are still missing) in the Vietnam War between 1959 and 1975.

Vietnam is a small country in Southeast Asia. American soldiers were sent there at a time when our country's leaders feared that communism would take over the world. At the war's peak, more than 500,000 Americans were fighting in Vietnam. But at home not all Americans supported this war—Vietnam divided Americans more than anything else since the Civil War.

The Vietnam Veterans Memorial was built to honor the war dead and missing and to heal the divisions in American society. It was designed by a 21-year-old college student, Maya Lin. Every year millions of people visit this memorial. Some trace the names of family members or friends. Others leave flowers or photos or keepsakes in memory of these men and women.

Try This

- How many people live in your community? Is this more or fewer than 58,000? Draw a bar graph to compare the size of your community with the number of Americans who died in the Vietnam War. Do library research to find the population of the United States, the population of Vietnam, and the number of Vietnamese who died in the war. Add these to your graph.

- People of your parents' age and older remember the Vietnam War. Interview some of them to find out how the war affected your community. Write some questions first, then use a tape recorder to capture the answers people give you. Share your interviews with your class.

Vietnam Veterans Memorial

Color and cut out the Vietnam Veterans Memorial. Fold up the base as shown. Glue the two pieces together. Line up the base tab with the angle and glue in place. Add it to your model of our nation's capital.

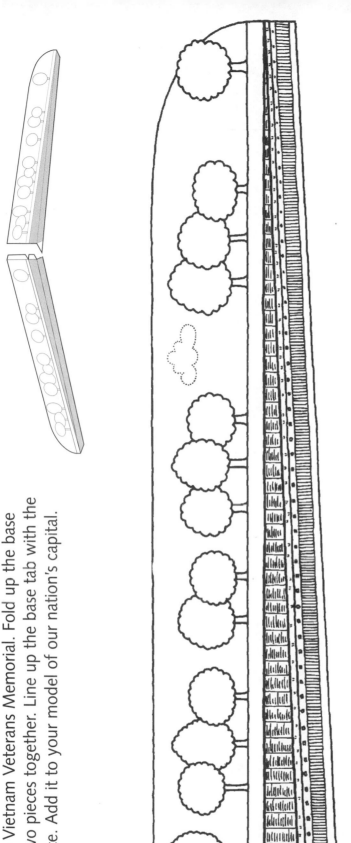

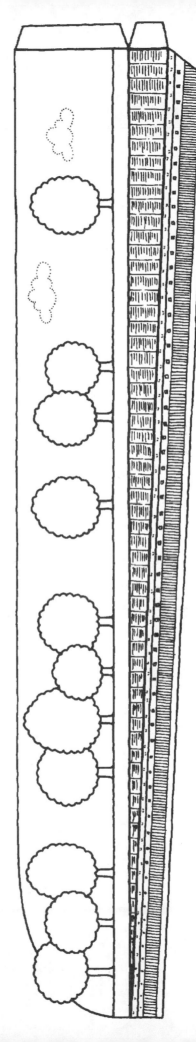

Family Tree

How far back can you trace your family? Fill in your name and the names of as many relatives as you can. Ask a family member to help you—you're likely to get some good family stories at the same time!

GRANDFATHER

Name:

_____

_____

Date Born:

_____

Where:

_____

GRANDMOTHER

Name:

_____

_____

Date Born:

_____

Where:

_____

GRANDFATHER

Name:

_____

_____

Date Born:

_____

Where:

_____

GRANDMOTHER

Name:

_____

_____

Date Born:

_____

Where:

_____

FATHER

Name: _____

Date Born: _____

Where: _____

MOTHER

Name: _____

Date Born: _____

Where: _____

ME

Name: _____

Date Born: _____

Where: _____

Some of Washington's Interesting People

From the beginning, Washington was filled with interesting people with wonderful stories to tell. Included here are four brief biographies of people who left their mark on Washington in the 18th, 19th, and 20th centuries. But don't stop there—encourage students to explore biographies of other people connected with Washington.

Each story in this section has a different format. You can suggest these formats as models for students when you ask them to write stories of other people they read about.

Activities

Benjamin Banneker

As the surveyor and mapmaker of Washington, D.C., Benjamin Banneker was the most famous African American of his day. But he was also an accomplished mathematician, astronomer, and writer.

Students can read his story as a small comic book (pages 39–42) if you duplicate it back-to-back, cut along the solid lines, and fold along the dotted lines. It has an easy reading level and drawings to reinforce the text.

You can use this as a critical reading puzzle. Cover the mini-book page numbers. Then duplicate the story on four separate pages (not back-to-back). Cut apart the blocks. Shuffle the story blocks and ask students to rearrange them in chronological order. To do so, students must read carefully for word clues about time and sequence. This is a good activity for small groups.

Clara Barton

Clara Barton was one of Washington's average citizens whose devotion to public service led to great humanitarian accomplishments. A clerk at the Patent Office when the Civil War broke out, she took it upon herself to provide the soldiers with supplies. She then became a battlefield nurse, and after the war went on to found the American Red Cross.

Her story on pages 43–48 is in the form of a readers' theater script. In readers' theater, students do not have to memorize their lines. They simply stand in front of their audience and read their parts with feeling.

The Cast of Characters calls for fourteen players. If you want to involve more students, the script calls for a number of sound effects. Recruit your nonactors to sound like balls whistling through the air, footsteps, doors opening and closing, horses' hooves, and lots of battlefield moans and groans.

Theodore Roosevelt

Teddy Roosevelt was one of our most colorful presidents. The youngest man ever to hold the job, he was famous for his use of the Oval Office as a bully pulpit to promote causes he believed in. One of the most important of these was environmental conservation.

The highlights of Roosevelt's life appear on pages 49–52 in a mini-book. Make it by photocopying the pages back-to-back. Give a sheet to each student, with the A-B-C-D side faceup. Students cut the panels apart along the three solid lines. Then they place the panels on top of each other in alphabetical order, with the panel marked A on top. To finish the book, students staple and fold the panels along the dashed line.

Maya Lin

At age 21, Maya Lin was one of the youngest people to make her mark on Washington with her design for the Vietnam Veterans Memorial. In contrast to all of the monuments to great leaders throughout Washington, Lin's work reflects the importance of individuals in our national experience.

This brief reading on pages 53–54 can lead to several writing experiences. Students might like to write to Maya Lin to ask questions about her work. They might also write a journal entry, short story, or poem as someone who has just visited the wall.

BOOK LINKS

Benjamin Banneker

- ✪ *Benjamin Banneker: The Man Who Saved Washington* by Claude Lewis (McGraw-Hill, 1970). Very well-written account of Banneker's whole life.
- ✪ *Dear Benjamin Banneker* by Andrea Davis Pinkney (Harcourt, 1994). Winner of the 1995 Carter G. Woodson Elementary Merit Award.

Clara Barton

- ✪ *Clara Barton: Angel of the Battlefield* by Rae Bains (Troll, 1982). Focuses on Barton's childhood and the forces shaping her character.
- ✪ *Clara Barton: Red Cross Pioneer* by Matthew G. Grant (Creative Education, 1974). For very young readers.
- ✪ *The Story of Clara Barton* by Zachary Kent (Children's Press, 1987). Highly readable, with great anecdotes and detail.

Theodore Roosevelt

- ✪ *Bully for You, Teddy Roosevelt!* by Jean Fritz (Putnam, 1991). A delightful read, full of fascinating details and anecdotes.
- ✪ *Theodore Roosevelt* by Eden Force (Franklin Watts, 1987). For somewhat younger readers.
- ✪ *Theodore Roosevelt Takes Charge* by Nancy Whitelaw (Albert Whitman, 1992). For more capable readers. Good photographs and illustrations.
- ✪ *Theodore Roosevelt: The Strenuous Life* by John Garraty and the editors of American Heritage (Harper, 1967). Part of the American Heritage Junior Library.

Benjamin Banneker published these letters as part of his almanac in 1792. It sold very well, and he updated it every year until 1802. He died in 1806, at the age of 75, and was buried on his farm. There is no headstone to mark his grave, but our nation's capital stands today as a monument to his great mind.

Benjamin Banneker

Today Washington, D.C., is one of the most beautiful cities in the world. It didn't just happen—it was planned that way. But it almost *didn't* happen, when the planner left town with his plans. The memory of an incredible man, Benjamin Banneker, rescued our nation's capital.

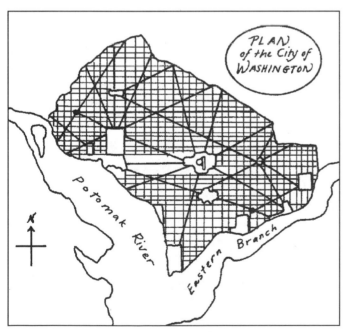

Using his notes and his memory, Benjamin restored L'Enfant's plans. Now workmen could start turning the swampy federal land into the beautiful capital of Washington, D.C. Benjamin Banneker became the best known black man in America.

As a boy, Ben was always curious about everything around him. He worked in the fields with his father and loved to learn new things. From his grandmother he learned how to read the Bible and how to do arithmetic. She always took him along when she went to the store— Ben could add faster and better than anybody.

Benjamin Banneker was born on November 9, 1731. He grew up on a tobacco plantation in Maryland, the son of Mary and Robert Banneker, who were free blacks. Ben's grandmother had come from England as an indentured servant. Ben's grandfather was the son of an African chief who had been enslaved.

But he did not rest on his success in Washington. He decided to write to Thomas Jefferson to point out that slavery was contrary to the principles of liberty and justice set forth in the Declaration of Independence. To Jefferson, a fellow scientist, he also sent a draft of his almanac. Jefferson quickly wrote back praising Banneker's work and agreeing that the condition of black people must be improved.

Going to school was a rare thing for most boys in those days, and it was almost unheard of for black children. But Ben's mother knew he was bright and should have an education. Quaker schoolmaster Peter Heinrich welcomed Ben to his class, and soon he was the best student.

Then Benjamin spoke up. He respected Jefferson for writing "all men are created equal" in the Declaration of Independence. But he also knew that Jefferson owned slaves. How would Jefferson treat him? Swallowing his fear, he offered to redraw the map from memory. Jefferson agreed to let him try.

When L'Enfant learned that he was fired, he stormed out of town and took all of his maps with him. Now this was really a crisis! Secretary of State Thomas Jefferson called together everyone who had been helping to plan the capital. How could they possibly solve this problem? The room was silent for a long time.

After he finished school, Ben went back to farming with his father. But he continued to learn and often borrowed books from his teacher. He became a kind of farmer scientist, always interested in how things work.

Andrew Ellicott suggested that Ben write an almanac. Farmers in those days relied on almanacs for information about stars, tides, and weather. Ben set about this new task with great energy. Soon Andrew had a new job too—chief surveyor for the nation's capital, which was to be built on the Potomac River. And who would be better to help him lay out the new federal city than his mathematician friend, Benjamin Banneker?

This clock made Benjamin Banneker famous. Now he traveled around Maryland fixing clocks and watches at the homes of wealthy people. How surprised they were to meet this educated and talented freeman!

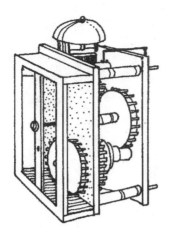

When Ben was about 30, his friend Joseph Levi showed him a watch. Ben was fascinated—he had never seen such a thing before. Joseph lent him the watch, and Ben took it apart and studied it carefully. Then he put it back together. Ever curious, he decided to make his own clock out of wood. It took a lot of work to carve the pieces to exactly the right shape and size. When it was finished, it was a masterpiece. It even chimed on the hour.

Ben jumped at the chance to work on the new city. He followed the head planner, Pierre-Charles L'Enfant, everywhere and took notes on everything. But L'Enfant was a stubborn man who would not accept any changes to his plans. When one of the city commissioners built a house where L'Enfant wanted to put a street, L'Enfant had the house torn down. President Washington was furious! He had the house rebuilt elsewhere, but now there was no way to work with L'Enfant.

On one of his trips to town, Benjamin met John, Andrew, and Joseph Ellicott. They were going to build a mill and a new town just up the river. Soon they became Ben's friends, and this friendship changed his life. He put together their mill machines, built a forge, helped build the town of Ellicott's Mill, and even surveyed its new road. Ben had never been busier or happier.

A few years later, one of the Ellicotts gave Benjamin a telescope and some books on astronomy. He taught himself how to look at the stars and understand the tables that explained their movements. But he suspected there were mistakes in the tables, and so he learned the difficult math he needed in order to correct them. When people learned what he had done, Benjamin's fame spread.

Clara Barton

CAST OF CHARACTERS

Narrator	Joe
Dr. Jay	Mr. Douglas
Mrs. Barton	Driver
David Barton	Sentry
Clara Barton	Dr. Dunn
Charles	Dr. Dubois
Pete	President Chester A. Arthur

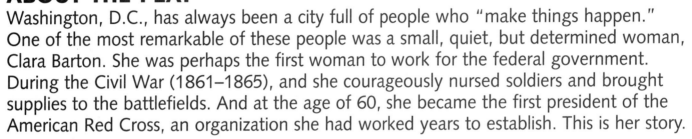

ABOUT THE PLAY

Washington, D.C., has always been a city full of people who "make things happen."
One of the most remarkable of these people was a small, quiet, but determined woman,
Clara Barton. She was perhaps the first woman to work for the federal government.
During the Civil War (1861–1865), and she courageously nursed soldiers and brought
supplies to the battlefields. And at the age of 60, she became the first president of the
American Red Cross, an organization she had worked years to establish. This is her story.

✪ Scene 1   *The Barton home in Massachusetts*

NARRATOR: Clara Barton was born in North Oxford, Massachusetts, in
1821, the youngest of five children. She was an eager student,
but at age 11 she stopped going to school to care for her injured
brother. Now, two years after his accident, the doctor visits the
Barton family.

DR. JAY: I came as soon as I got your message, Mrs. Barton. Has David
taken a turn for the worse? It's been two years since his terrible
fall from the barn. How is he doing?

MRS. BARTON: See for yourself, Doctor.

DAVID: Hello, Doctor! Bet you never thought you'd see me up and
around again.

DR. JAY: David, just look at you—what a miracle!

DAVID: No miracle, Doctor. My little sister, Clara, has taken care of me
night and day all this time.

DR. JAY: Clara, you have a natural gift for nursing.

CLARA: Thank you, Doctor.

✪ Scene 2 *A schoolroom*

NARRATOR: Clara went back to school when David was well. At age 17 she decided to become a teacher. Today she faces her first class, full of tough 14-year-old bullies.

CLARA: Good morning, class. I am Miss Barton, your new teacher.

CHARLES: Psst, Pete. Let's scare her off, just like the last one.

CLARA: No talking, please. We'll begin with geography. Who can name our nation's capital?

PETE: Who cares, little missy?

(Sound Effects: class laughter)

CLARA: It seems you don't like the rules of the classroom, young man. Very well, we'll play by the rules of the schoolyard. Whoever can throw a ball the farthest will be in charge of this class. Come outside!

(Sound Effects: footsteps, door opening and closing, more footsteps)

CHARLES *(grunts as he throws ball):* There! I'd like to see anybody beat that!

(Sound Effects: ball whistling through the air)

PETE: So there, big shot. What do you think of that?

CLARA: My turn.

(Sound Effects: ball whistling through the air for a long time)

JOE: Gosh, Miss Barton, yours went farther than any of ours.

PETE: I'm sorry, Miss Barton. We were just trying to scare you off, like our last teacher. But now we gotta respect anyone who's so good an athlete!

⭐ Scene 3 *U.S. Patent Office in Washington, D.C.*

NARRATOR: Clara taught school in Massachusetts and New Jersey for about 15 years. In 1854 she decided it was time for a change and moved to Washington, D.C. There she got a job in the U.S. Patent Office. Now it is 1862, and she is leaving that job.

MR. DOUGLAS: Miss Barton, I understand you want to leave the Patent Office. You were the first woman to work here, maybe even the first woman in the federal government. Your work has been excellent, and we really depend on you. Why are you going?

CLARA: It's for our soldiers, sir. The Civil War has been going on for a year, and our soldiers desperately need supplies. At first I gathered towels and handkerchiefs and such for them and gave them out to soldiers on their way to the front. Then I began writing to families for things the soldiers need, like blankets and candles. My apartment turned into a warehouse! But things are much worse now, with so many wounded. I've got permission from the army to deliver nursing supplies to the battlefield.

MR. DOUGLAS: It's a dangerous job for anyone, but if anyone can do it, it's you. I wish you well, Miss Barton.

CLARA: Thank you, sir.

✪ Scene 4 *Near a Civil War battlefield*

NARRATOR: A few days later, the Battle of Cedar Mountain was fought in Virginia. Clara knew that soldiers were left suffering on the battlefield. With her written passes from the army, she loaded a wagon with nursing supplies and went there to help.

DRIVER: Miss Barton, It's nearly midnight. You sure you want to make it to the battlefield tonight? It would be easier to find our way at sunup.

CLARA: But the suffering and the hunger don't stop at night. We must push on.

(Sound Effects: horse clip-clopping, moans and cries of pain)

SENTRY: Halt! Who goes there?

CLARA: Clara Barton, with nursing supplies from the Union Army. Please take me to your field surgeon.

SENTRY: Dr. Dunn, this lady says she has supplies for you.

CLARA: Indeed I do, sir. Dressings and bandages, shirts, food. And I will stay to help hand out these supplies and make soup for all.

DR. DUNN: If ever heaven sent out an angel, it is you, Miss Barton— the Angel of the Battlefield.

✪ Scene 5 *Clara's home*

NARRATOR: Clara continued to go wherever she was needed, bringing supplies and nursing the wounded. Her motto was, "Ease pain, soothe sorrow, lessen suffering." After her service at many battles, General Benjamin Butler asked her to supervise all the nurses of the Union Army. It was a huge task. One night she makes time to write to a friend.

CLARA *(Writing):* You would not believe what an average day is like for me. Today, among other things, I have cooked ten dozen eggs, washed hands and feet, put ice on hot heads, mustard on cold feet, written six soldiers' letters home, stood beside three death beds . . . and now at this hour, midnight, I am too sleepy and stupid to write. If we cannot put an end to war, we must find a better way to care for our soldiers.

✪ Scene 6 *A Swiss hospital*

NARRATOR: After the war, Clara gave lectures on her battlefield experiences. When her voice gave out, she went to Europe to rest and recover. There she learned about the Red Cross, founded in Switzerland in 1864. When the Franco-Prussian War broke out in 1870, she again volunteered to help.

CLARA: Bonjour, Doctor. I am Clara Barton. I supervised nurses in the American Civil War, and I would like to help out here.

DR. DUBOIS: Thank you so much, Miss Barton. Let me show you our hospital and find you something to do.

(Sound Effects: door opens and closes; footsteps)

DR. DUBOIS: Here is our main ward.

CLARA: Why, this is unbelievable! All that bloodshed on the battlefield, but here everything is orderly and clean. No lack of bandages or food or nurses. How is it possible that you have reduced wartime suffering so much?

DR. DUBOIS: It is all the work of the Red Cross, relief societies that were organized during peacetime to provide care for the wounded when war came again. Not a bad idea, eh?

CLARA: I must do everything in my power to bring the Red Cross to America.

✪ Scene 7 *(The White House)*

NARRATOR: Clara returned to the United States in 1873 and threw her energies into setting up the Red Cross here. To do so, she had to talk to senators and congressmen and even three presidents. Now it is 1882, and Clara has been called to the crowded office of President Chester A. Arthur.

PRESIDENT ARTHUR: Ladies and gentlemen, I have called you here today for a very important occasion. Today I am authorizing the establishment of the American Red Cross. This organization will provide relief not only for soldiers in wartime but also for civilians in times of disaster. The Red Cross will improve the lives and well-being of all Americans. As first president of the American Red Cross, I name Miss Clara Barton, who was well known as "the Angel of the Battlefield" during the Civil War. Her tireless efforts have brought this worthy organization into being. We owe her enormous thanks.

CLARA: Thank you, Mr. President, for your kind words. But seeing the good work of the American Red Cross will be all the thanks I could ever ask for.

NARRATOR: Clara Barton served as president of the American Red Cross at its headquarters in Washington, D.C., until 1904. During that time, the Red Cross helped thousands of people after earthquakes, storms, and floods and cared for soldiers during the Spanish-American War. Reluctantly, Clara retired at the age of 83. She lived to be 90 years old and left behind a shining example of caring and public service.

The Life of
Theodore Roosevelt

Teddy Roosevelt was born in New York in 1858. As a child, he suffered from asthma. His father told him he must "make his body," so Teddy worked out in his own gym. While he built up his strength, he also learned how to overcome things that stood in his way.

A

Teddy Roosevelt was the 26th President of the United States. He loved adventure and the out-of-doors, and he devoted his life to public service.

B

As President, Theodore Roosevelt worked to give every American a "square deal." He believed in fairness and good government for all.

From an early age, Teddy loved animals and nature. He collected all sorts of creatures for his "Roosevelt Museum of Natural History." But his mother drew the line at a litter of dead field mice in the ice box.

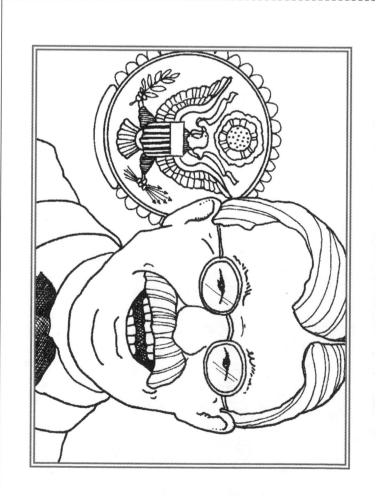

Teddy went to Harvard College. After graduation he entered Columbia Law School. But soon he was elected to the New York State Assembly (law-making body). He gave up studying law for a career in politics and public service.

C

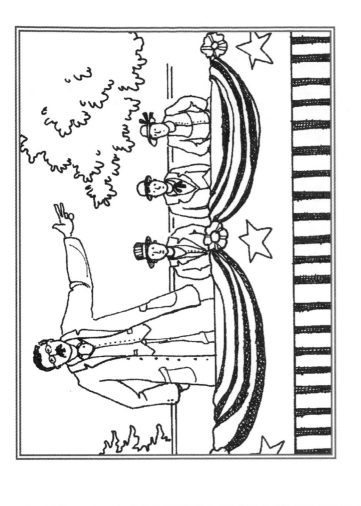

Roosevelt was known as the "Conservation President" because he set up national forests, parks, and wildlife preserves. Did you know that the teddy bear was named for him? Once, when hunting, he refused to shoot a bear cub. A toy-maker made a stuffed bear and named it Teddy. Teddy bears have been popular ever since.

D

In 1900 Roosevelt was elected Vice President of the United States. When President McKinley was killed in 1901, Roosevelt became President. At 42, he was the youngest man ever to hold the job. With his wife and six children, Roosevelt moved to the White House. He was elected President in 1904.

51

After three terms in the State Assembly, Teddy became a rancher in North Dakota. He loved the West and learned the importance of preserving wilderness areas.

After a terrible winter killed his cattle, Teddy left the ranch and held several important jobs in Washington. When the Spanish-American War broke out in 1898, he formed a regiment called the Rough Riders. He led the charge up San Juan Hill in Cuba and became a hero. Returning to New York, Roosevelt was elected governor.

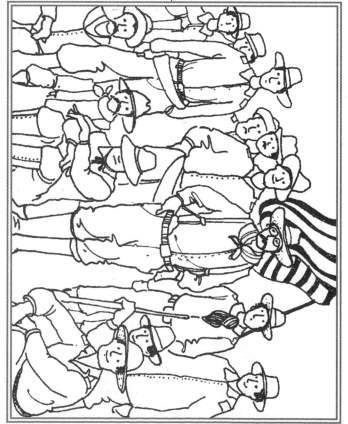

Maya Lin

What is the most frequently visited monument in Washington and indeed the whole United States? It is the Vietnam Veterans Memorial on the Mall, near the Lincoln Memorial. You might think that the government asked a world-famous artist to design it. But in fact, a veterans' group held a contest for the best design, and the winner was a 21-year-old college student, Maya Lin.

Maya grew up in Athens, Ohio, the daughter of college teachers. Her parents came to the United States from China in 1949. As a child, Maya loved to read and do math and make things. She even built little towns in her room. In high school she was tops in her class and was admitted to Yale University.

In college Maya studied architecture. During her last year, she saw a poster about the contest for the Vietnam Veterans Memorial. Even though she didn't know much about the war, she decided to enter the contest.

Most monuments honor a victory or a hero. Maya wanted, instead, to help people overcome the pain of losing someone they knew in the war. To make it personal, she focused her work on all the names of those who had died.

Her design was entry 1,026 out of more than 1,420. No one was more surprised than Maya when she won. Yet there were many people who did not like her work and argued bitterly against it, calling it an ugly black wall. Some did not like the fact that she was an Asian American, or that she was a woman, or that she had not served in the war. Instead of healing the nation, Maya's design seemed to be stirring up new trouble.

But when the Vietnam Veterans Memorial was built, it touched people just the way Maya had intended it to. Its purpose, she says, was "to help the veterans coming back, to help their families, to talk to people one hundred years from now who will know nothing about that war and nobody on that wall. To me, it's a very simple notion: you cannot ever forget that war is not just a victory or a loss. It's really about individual lives."

The millions of people who visit the Vietnam wall each year agree with her. Thanks to Maya Lin, visitors to Washington can experience a personal connection to our nation's very recent past. Her vision helps us to see American history as the stories of individual men and women.

Washington, D.C., Metro Game

The Metro Game is a great way for students to review what they have learned about Washington, D.C. All of the questions on pages 57–64 are based on information presented through the activities in this book. But don't stop there! You can adapt the game to what your own class has done. Adding custom-made questions also enables you to tailor the game to the needs and abilities of your students. Six students or six teams of students can play the game.

How to Make the Game:

1. Place the poster (bound in the back of the book) on a flat surface. Reproduce pages 56–64.

2. The spinner will show where each player will start. To make it, paste the spinner and arrow on page 64 to cardboard and cut out the circle and arrow. Color each section according to the color of the subway line. Attach the arrow to the center of the circle with a brass fastener. Make sure the arrow can spin.

3. Cut out the cards on pages 57–64. Fold them on the dashed line so the question is on one side and the answer is on the other side. Tape the open ends. Shuffle them and stack them in a pile with the questions facing up, the answers facing down. The WildCards should have that word faceup and the consequences facedown.

4. Provide students with a copy of the game directions on page 56. Encourage them to create more question cards to try to stump their friends based on what they've learned and researched. They can also make some more WildCards—the wilder the better!

Other Ideas:

✪ You may want to add map-reading skills to the questions. For example, you might write question cards such as "Which stop is directly north of Smithsonian?" and "Which stop is the next stop southeast of Woodley Park–Zoo?" WildCards might send players to specific stops all over the board.

✪ Encourage students to write their own question cards. If students have done individual or small-group projects, they can base their questions on them.

✪ You may want to challenge older students to make the game more complex by adding different levels of difficulty to their questions. For example, students could write level 3 questions to advance three stops, level 2 questions to advance two stops, and level 1 questions to advance one stop. The catch here is that a *wrong* answer sends the player back an equivalent number of stops.

✪ Just for fun, have students play the game backward, reading the answer on the card first and then having to ask the right question.

🏠 **Hometown Connection** Students may enjoy making a similar game for their own community. You can use a bus map as the basis for a game board. This is a good opportunity to talk about the benefits of mass transit.

The Washington, D.C., Metro Game

There's so much to see and do in Washington, D.C., that it is very hard to walk everywhere. Fortunately, there's a wonderful subway system called the Metro that whisks people from place to place quickly and quietly (the cars run on rubber wheels). The Metro also helps the environment—people taking the subway are not driving their cars and polluting the air. You can use the map of the Metro for a game board about Washington, D.C.

HOW TO PLAY:

The object of the game is to get to the Capitol South stop on either the blue or orange line of the Metro. You will have to read the map and figure out where to change trains to get there.

✪ To start the game, each player spins to find out which Metro to get on. (If you spin a place that someone else has already taken, spin again.)

✪ Take turns answering questions in the pile. A right answer advances you to the next stop on the Metro. A wrong answer keeps you where you are until the next turn.

✪ WildCards can help you go forward or back on your trip to the Capitol. Some can even send you to a different part of the game board.

✪ The winner is the first person to reach the Capitol.

Metro Game Cards

Where did Dr. Martin Luther King deliver his "I Have a Dream" speech?	the Lincoln Memorial	Who wrote the Declaration of Independence?	Thomas Jefferson
Why is the President's house called the White House?	It was given many coats of white paint after a fire during the War of 1812.	Who was the Great Emancipator? How did he get that name?	Abraham Lincoln, who emancipated, or freed, the slaves
What is the oldest official building in Washington?	the White House	Who was the first President to live in the White House?	John Adams
Who were the first people to live in the area of Washington, D.C.?	the Piscataway	Who designed the plan for the city?	Pierre-Charles L'Enfant

Metro Game Cards

How many members does the Senate have?	100
What does Congress do?	It makes laws for our country.
How did the Washington Monument lose one of its steps?	It was converted into a wheelchair ramp.
Who was "first in war, first in peace, first in the hearts of his countrymen"?	George Washington

How many members does the House of Representatives have?	435
What are the two parts of Congress?	the Senate and the House of Representatives
What is the purpose of the Capitol building?	It is where Congress meets.
What is the tallest stone building in the world?	the Washington Monument

Metro Game Cards

Where in Washington does it say "Equal Justice Under Law"?	over the front doors of the Supreme Court	What is the Supreme Court?	the highest court in the land
Which Washington museum contains George Washington's uniform?	the National Museum of American History	Where in Washington can you touch a moon rock?	the National Air and Space Museum
The National Air and Space Museum is part of what organization?	the Smithsonian Institution	How did the Smithsonian Institution get started?	James Smithson left money for an organization that would spread knowledge.
How many Senators does each state send to Congress?	two	How many Representatives does each state send to Congress?	The number of representatives depends on the state's population.

Metro Game Cards

Where is American paper money printed?

the Bureau of Engraving and Printing

How many trees are cut down to make the paper for dollar bills?

None. The paper is made of cotton and linen.

Where are America's important documents stored?

the National Archives

What does the National Archives store in helium-filled glass cases?

the original Declaration of Independence, Constitution, Bill of Rights

What is the Constitution of the United States?

It is the highest law of the land and sets up the federal government.

What was Brown v. Board of Education?

a Supreme Court decision that said school segregation was unconstitutional

What does the Supreme Court do?

It decides whether state laws, acts of Congress, and actions by the President are constitutional.

Who wrote the Gettysburg Address?

Abraham Lincoln

Metro Game Cards

What building sits on Jenkin's Hill in Washington, D.C.?

the Capitol

Where can you see the largest diamond in the world?

the National Museum of Natural History

Which President doubled the size of the United States?

Thomas Jefferson

Who was the only President ever elected unanimously?

George Washington

What were the two reasons for building the Vietnam Veterans Memorial?

to honor the war dead and to heal the divisions in American society

Where does the President have his office?

in the White House

Who designed the Vietnam Veterans Memorial? How old was this designer?

Maya Lin; she was 21.

How many names are carved into the Vietnam Veterans Memorial?

more than 58,000

Metro Game Cards

What contribution did Benjamin Banneker make to Washington, D.C.?	What organization did Clara Barton help to found?	What kind of a book did Benjamin Banneker write?
He surveyed the land and drew the map of the city from memory.	American Red Cross	an almanac
How did the teddy bear get its name?	Clara Barton was the first woman to work in which federal office?	Who was called the "Angel of the Battlefield" and why?
from President Teddy Roosevelt, who refused to shoot a bear cub	U.S. Patent Office	Clara Barton, because she cared for soldiers during the Civil War
Who was the youngest man ever to be elected President?	How did President Theodore Roosevelt help the environment?	
Theodore Roosevelt	He set up national forests, parks, and wildlife preserves.	

62